POLITICAL
Animals

GW00706068

POLITICAL ANIMALS
A New Internationalist BOOK TO GO

Published by New Internationalist Publications Ltd
55 Rectory Road
Oxford OX4 1BW
www.newint.org
New Internationalist is a registered trademark

Cover image by Firefly Productions/Corbis.
Credits for other images on Page 190.

Compiled by Bev Laing

Designed/Edited by Alan Hughes/Chris Brazier.

Printed on recycled paper by South China Printing Co Ltd,
Hong Kong, China.

British Library Cataloguing-in-Publication Data.
A catalogue record for this book is available from the British Library.

ISBN 1 904456 24 3

Introduction

HAVE A LOOK at any major political debate and you will soon spot braying donkeys, quick-tongued snakes and clucking hens – usually making a great deal of noise.

The wily fox, the wise owl... for all that we humans might assert the difference between us and animals, we keep turning to animal comparisons to explain our behaviour and that of our politicians. Throughout political history, animals have borne the burden of our metaphors in the pithy comments we choose to make about our elected (and unelected) leaders.

But there is a more deadly side to our relationship with the creatures that share our planet – cruelty, exploitation and, in all too many cases, extinction. There is no doubt that nature is red in tooth and claw. But if you would like to come face to face with the most dangerous animal of all – just look in the mirror!

Alan Hughes

Note: old quotations using 'man' as a generic term for all people have generally been adapted to accord with modern usage.

HUMANS ARE BY NATURE POLITICAL ANIMALS.

Aristotle (384-322 BCE), Greek philosopher

Now I know what a statesman is;
he's a dead politician.

Bob Edwards (1865-1922), Canadian journalist

We need more

statesmen.

9

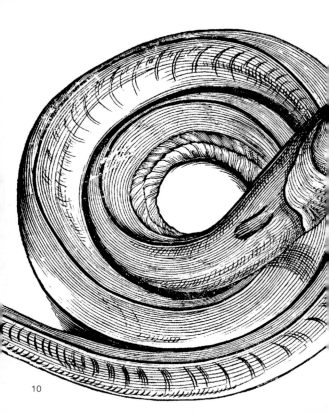

10

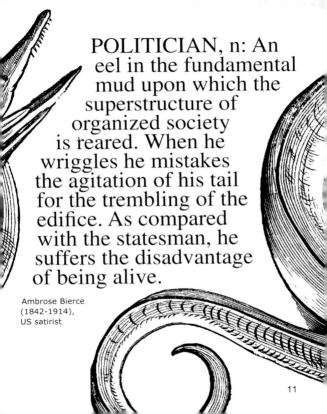

POLITICIAN, n: An eel in the fundamental mud upon which the superstructure of organized society is reared. When he wriggles he mistakes the agitation of his tail for the trembling of the edifice. As compared with the statesman, he suffers the disadvantage of being alive.

Ambrose Bierce
(1842-1914),
US satirist

11

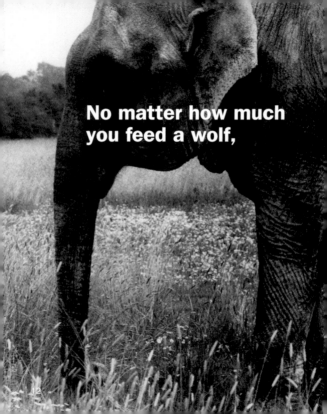

No matter how much
you feed a wolf,

an elephant
still has
bigger
BALLS.

Russian popular saying

13

Under every stone lurks a politician.

Aristophanes (456-380 BCE), Greek dramatist

14

People can be as greedy as a snake trying to swallow an elephant.

Chinese proverb

15

A little more matriarchy is what the world needs, and I know it. Period. Paragraph.

Dorothy Thompson
(1893-1961), US journalist

Mosquitos are the **fattest** inhabitants of this republic.

Fred D'Aguiar (1960-), Guyanan writer

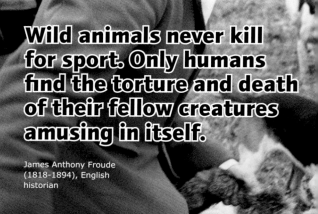

Wild animals never kill for sport. Only humans find the torture and death of their fellow creatures amusing in itself.

James Anthony Froude
(1818-1894), English
historian

21

a politician is an arse upon...

...which everyone has sat except a man.

e e cummings (1894-1962), US poet

22

The species we endanger today are like the canaries put down mines to warn against poisonous gases. As we destroy and reshape habitat locally and globally we will in the end be our own victims. Not only will we be creating a soulless place, devoid of birdsong with ever-expanding vistas of plastic and concrete, but the biodiversity we need to protect our bodies and sustain our spirits is the one thing that we can never replace.

Richard Swift (1946-), Canadian journalist

The problem with political jokes is that they get elected.

Henry Cate VII

They politics like ours profess,
The greater play upon the less.

Matthew Green (1696-1737), English poet

29

It is curious how there seems to be an instinctive disgust in humans for their nearest ancestors and relations. If only Darwin could conscientiously have traced humans back to the Elephant or the Lion or the Antelope, how much ridicule and prejudice would have been spared to the doctrine of Evolution.

Havelock Ellis (1859-1939), British psychologist

EXTINCTION IS FOREVER

The lengthening roll-call of species that are no longer with us is truly alarming. In the past, human intervention through hunting and harvesting was the main culprit in eliminating entire, often quite numerous, species. While this is still a problem, the shaping of natural habitat for everything from cars to crops is today the main threat to other species, particularly in the tropics and the wetlands.

Mastodon

This huge herbivore was once held to be the victim of climate change. Now many of the mega-fauna (like sabre-tooth tigers) of the Americas are thought to have fallen to the experienced hunters of Euro-Asia. The Mastodon did not have the time to adapt to the world's most efficient predator.

Passenger Pigeon

Last seen in 1889, flocks of these bright-eyed wild pigeons once darkened the skies of eastern North America, recorded in flocks five or six kilometres wide. But they proved easy prey for commercial hunters.

Palestinian Painted Frog

This colourful frog lived mostly in the area of Lake Hula on the Syrian-Israeli border. The last one died in 1956. It is one of a number of species that have vanished due to drainage and wetland modification schemes.

Moa

These large flightless birds were no match for Maori hunters in New Zealand / Aotearoa. An environment without predators was suddenly invaded by humans and their egg-gobbling fellow traveller, the common rat.

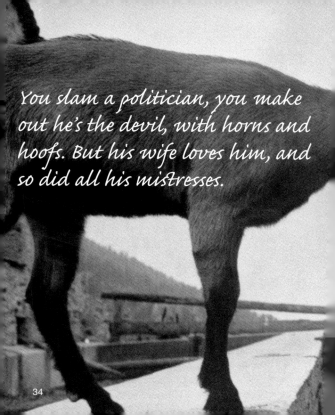

You slam a politician, you make out he's the devil, with horns and hoofs. But his wife loves him, and so did all his mistresses.

34

Pamela Hansford Johnson
(1912-1981), English
dramatist

35

I do not see a delegation for the Four Footed. I see no seat for the Eagles. We forget and we consider ourselves superior.

But we are after all a mere part of Creation. And we must consider to understand where we are. And we stand somewhere between the mountain and the Ant. Somewhere and only there as part and parcel of the Creation.

Chief Oren Lyons (1930-), of the Onondaga Nation in the Iroquois Confederacy

**NOTHING
IS SO
ABJECT AND
PATHETIC**

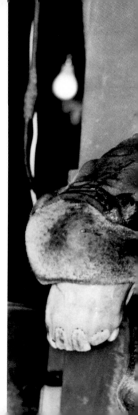

**AS A POLITICIAN
WHO HAS LOST
HIS JOB,**

SAVE
ONLY A
RETIRED
STUD-
HORSE.

Henry Louis Mencken (1880-1956), US journalist

It is easier for the
proverbial camel
to pass through
the needle's
eye,

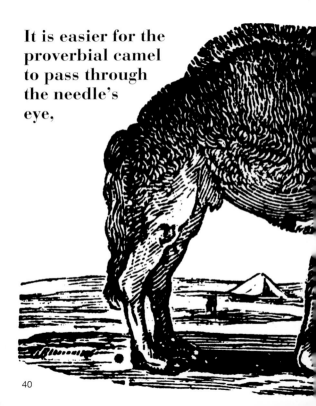

hump and all,

than
for an
erstwhile
colonial
administration
to give sound
and honest counsel
of a political nature to
its liberated territory.

Kwame Nkrumah (1909-1972),
Ghana's independence leader

People are born free, and are everywhere in chains.

Jean-Jacques Rousseau
(1712-1778), French philosopher

IT'S BETTER TO BE A LION FOR A DAY

**than a
sheep all
your life.**

Elizabeth Kenny
(1880-1952),
Australian nurse

A little **rebellion** now and then is a good thing.

Thomas Jefferson (1743-1826), US independence leader and president

47

The animals of the world exist for their own reasons.

They were not made for humans

any more than black people were made for white,

or women created for men.

Alice Walker (1944-), African-American writer

ALL ANIMALS ARE EQUAL BUT SOME ANIMALS ARE MORE EQUAL THAN OTHERS.

George Orwell (1903-1950), English novelist and essayist

IT
IS
BETTER
FOR
CIVILIZATION
TO
BE
GOING
DOWN
THE
DRAIN
THAN
TO
BE
COMING
UP IT.

Henry Allen (contemporary), US critic

THE EXTINCTION FILES

One of the better-known species we have driven to the edge of oblivion.

Beluga Whale
(Delphinapterus leucas)
HABITAT: One of the smallest whales, 4-6 metres long, with adults easily identified by creamy-white skin. Arctic Belugas are threatened (Hudson Bay) or endangered (Ungava Bay) but those in Quebec's St Lawrence River are most in peril.
NUMBERS: A century ago there were 5,000 St Lawrence Belugas. Today's population of approximately 500 is dangerously low.
THREAT: Habitat destruction and reduced food stocks derive from hydroelectric projects and commercial fishing, toxins from boating, extensive dredging, municipal sewage and industrial waste. High concentrations of chemicals and heavy metals have been found in Beluga carcasses since 1982.
CONSERVATION: Hunting was banned in 1979 but pollution remains a grave threat despite a clean-up launched in 1988. St Lawrence Beluga numbers may be too low to recover.

Disbelief in magic...

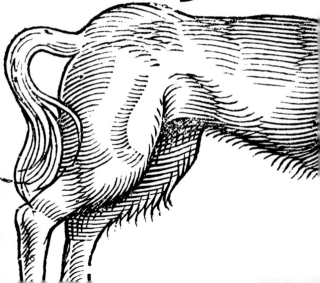

...can force a poor soul into believing in government and business.

Tom Robbins (1936-), US writer

A CONSERVATIVE IS A MAN WHO SITS AND THINKS, MOSTLY SITS.

Woodrow Wilson (1856-1924), US president

IF YOU T
ARE TOO
TO MAKE
DIFFERE
SLEEPIN
MOSQUI

INK YOU

SMALL

A

CE, TRY

WITH A

O.

Tensing Gyatso (1935-),
current Tibetan Dalai Lama

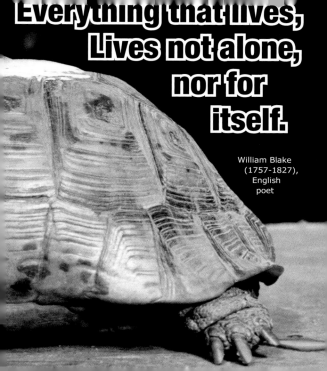

Everything that lives,
Lives not alone,
nor for
itself.

William Blake
(1757-1827),
English
poet

Fate is not an eagle,

it creeps like a rat.

Elizabeth Bowen (1899-1973), Irish novelist

In a world in which women, like other animals, are raped, mutilated and murdered by men, the woman who is given the skins of dead animals by her male 'protector' is being warned of his power at the same time as she is reassured of his patronage. The implicit threat serves as reminder of her own tenuous safety in a man's world.

Celia Kitzinger (contemporary), English social psychologist

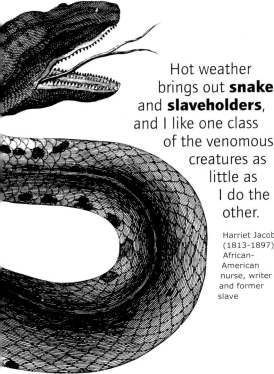

Hot weather brings out **snakes** and **slaveholders**, and I like one class of the venomous creatures as little as I do the other.

Harriet Jacobs (1813-1897), African-American nurse, writer and former slave

69

THE EXTINCTION FILES

One of the better-known species we have driven to the edge of oblivion.

Mountain Gorilla

(Gorilla gorilla berengei)
HABITAT: All three subspecies of gorillas are threatened, but none as perilously as mountain gorillas which live in the Virunga volcanoes region of Rwanda, Uganda and DR Congo. The largest living primate, it is thought to be the most intelligent land animal next to humans. Infant-mortality rates average about 45 per cent.
NUMBERS: Estimated at less than 400 surviving in the wild.
THREAT: The gorilla was first endangered when it was hunted for food. Currently the most serious threat is habitat destruction from human encroachment. Political unrest threatens conservation projects.
CONSERVATION: Trade restrictions have diminished hunting for capture, but laws control rather than prohibit trade in wild gorillas. Uganda's Bwindi Forest Reserve protects gorillas and their habitat.

The time will come when people will look upon the murder of animals as they now look upon the murder of men.

Leonardo Da Vinci (1452-1519),
Italian scientist, engineer and artist

*Get thee glass eyes;
And, like a scurvy
politician, seem
To see the things
thou dost not.*

William Shakespeare (1564-1616),
English dramatist, from *King Lear*

There is no such thing as a perfect leader either in the past or present, in China or elsewhere. If there is one, he is only pretending, like a pig inserting scallions into its nose in an effort to look like an elephant.

Liu Shao-Ch'i (1898-1969), Chinese communist leader

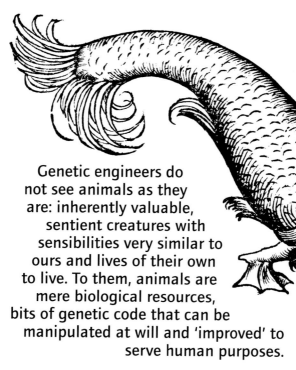

Genetic engineers do
not see animals as they
are: inherently valuable,
sentient creatures with
sensibilities very similar to
ours and lives of their own
to live. To them, animals are
mere biological resources,
bits of genetic code that can be
manipulated at will and 'improved' to
serve human purposes.

They can then be patented like a new toaster or tennis ball.

Carol Grunewald (contemporary),
US environmental activist and writer

Unity in a movement situation is overrated. If you were the Establishment, which would you rather see coming in the door, five hundred mice or one lion?

Florynce R Kennedy (1916-2001),
African-American lawyer and civil rights activist

From the **POINT OF VIEW** of the **INDIANS** of the Caribbean islands, **CHRISTOPHER COLUMBUS**, with his **PLUMED CAP** and **RED VELVET CAPE**, was the biggest **PARROT** they had **EVER SEEN**

Eduardo Galeano (1940-), Uruguayan historian and essayist

FROM the point of view of the **NATIVES**, it's the **TOURISTS** who are **PICTURESQUE**.

THE WHITE MEN WERE MANY AND WE COULD NOT HOLD OUR OWN WITH THEM. WE WERE LIKE DEER. THEY WERE LIKE GRIZZLY BEARS.

'Chief Joseph' or Hin-mah-too-yah-lat-kekt (1840-1904)
of the Nez Percé Native Americans

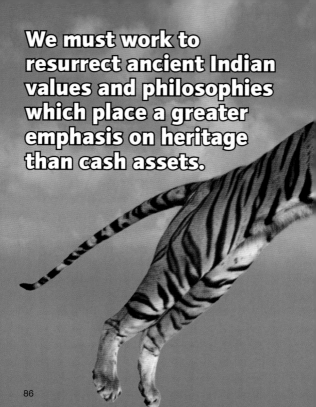

We must work to resurrect ancient Indian values and philosophies which place a greater emphasis on heritage than cash assets.

If we fail, the tiger will be lost to the world because India is its last stronghold. And if the tiger goes, with it will vanish the very soul of India.

Bittu Sahgal (contemporary), Indian ecologist

We call them dumb animals, and so they are, for they cannot tell us how they feel, but they do not suffer less because they have no words.

Anna Sewell (1820-1878),
English writer

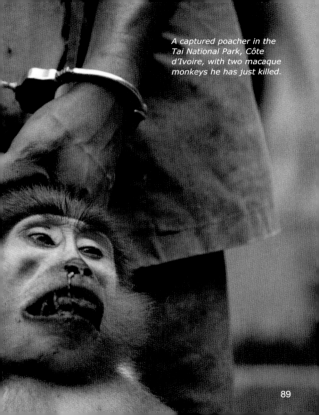

A captured poacher in the Tai National Park, Côte d'Ivoire, with two macaque monkeys he has just killed.

89

I am a red man. If the Great Spirit had desired me to be a white man he would have made me so in the first place. He put in your heart certain wishes and plans, in my heart he put other and different desires. Each man is good in his sight. It is not necessary for Eagles to be Crows. We are poor... but we are free. No white man controls our footsteps. If we must die... we die defending our rights.

Sitting Bull (1831-1890), Hunkpapa Lakota chief

POWER
corrupts,

but absolute **POWER** corrupts absolutely.

Emerich Edward Dalberg, Lord Acton
(1834-1902), British historian

NO SELF-RESPECTING FISH WOULD BE WRAPPED IN A MURDOCH NEWSPAPER.

Mike Royko (1932-1997), US journalist

Everybody **knows** that the **WHALE** is **smarter** than **we**

Probably that's why we call him the

king of the sea

We're killing **everything** on dry land, why don't we just let the **fishes** be?

Some of us are Greenpeace Warriors of the Sea

Joan Baez (1941-), US folk singer and activist

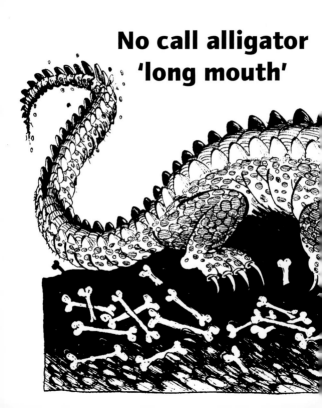

No call alligator 'long mouth'

– until you pass him.

US slave saying

Diplomacy is the art of saying 'Nice doggie' until you can find a rock.

Will Rogers (1879-1935), US humorist

I loathe people who keep dogs. They are cowards who haven't got the guts to bite people themselves.

August Strindberg (1849-1912), Swedish playwright and essayist

In extending our moral concern beyond the boundaries of our own species,

so as to respect the consciousness of all sentient individuals,

we are tackling the most IMPORTANT MORAL issue of the millennium.

Richard Ryder (contemporary),
British psychologist and
campaigner against speciesism

103

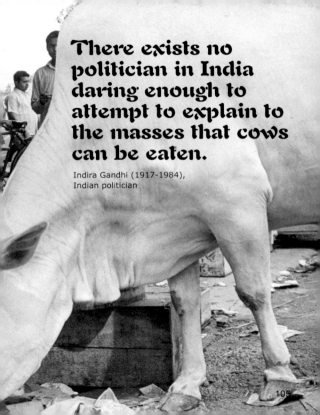

There exists no politician in India daring enough to attempt to explain to the masses that cows can be eaten.

Indira Gandhi (1917-1984),
Indian politician

105

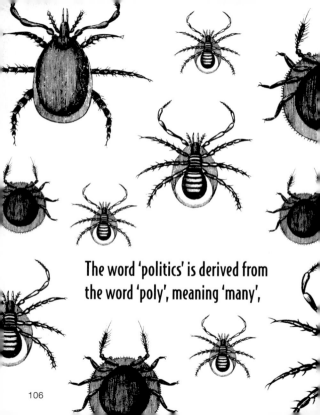

The word 'politics' is derived from the word 'poly', meaning 'many',

106

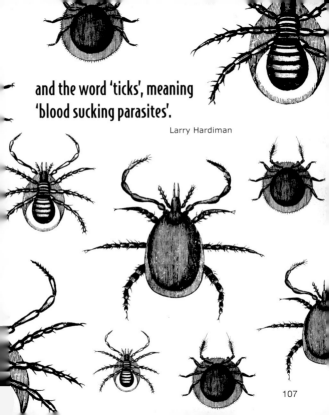

and the word 'ticks', meaning 'blood sucking parasites'.

Larry Hardiman

Circus dogs jump when the trainer cracks the whip, but the really well-trained dog is the one that turns somersaults when there is no whip.

George Orwell (1903-1950),
English novelist and essayist

I only want to ride the wind and walk the waves, slay the big whale of the eastern sea, clean up the frontiers and save the people from drowning.

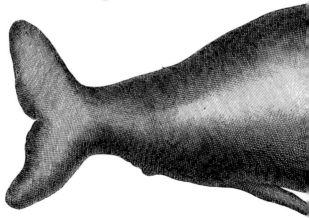

Why should I imitate others, bow my head, stoop over and be a slave? Why resign myself to menial housework?

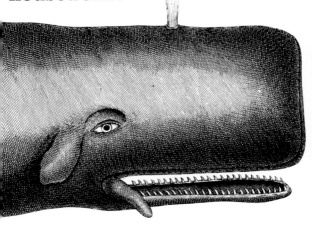

Trieu Thi Trinh, a Vietnamese peasant woman who led the resistance to Chinese invaders in the third century.

THE EXTINCTION FILES

One of the better-known species we have driven to the edge of oblivion.

Przewalski's Horse

(Equus przewalski)

HABITAT: This last truly wild horse is probably now extinct in the wild, although there may be a population in north-eastern Xinjiang, China. The last wild sighting was in 1966. It prefers open grassland, steppe and semi-desert. Przewalski's Horse differs from domestic horses in that it sheds its erect, long-haired mane.

NUMBERS: Over 1,000 are captive-bred in zoos and reserves.

THREAT: Hunting and loss of grazing land to domestic stock.

CONSERVATION: Captive populations derive from animals captured 80-100 years ago and have lost genetic diversity from years of inbreeding. But a long-term programme to reintroduce horses to the wild in Mongolia is meeting with some success.

A CHIEF REIGNS OVER HYENAS AND CROCODILES

AS WELL AS OVER USEFUL ANIMALS.

Tsonga (Mozambican) proverb

Oh! It is excellent To have a giant's strength, but it is tyrannous To use it like a giant.

William Shakespeare (1564-1616), English dramatist, from *Measure for Measure*

God loved the birds and invented trees. Humans loved the birds and invented cages.

Jacques Deval (1890-1972), French dramatist and filmmaker

I know why the caged bird sings.

Paul Laurence Dunbar (1872-1906), African-American poet

British King George VI meets his match.

I like pigs. Dogs look up to us. Cats look down on us. Pigs treat us as equals.

Sir Winston Churchill (1874-1965), British prime minister

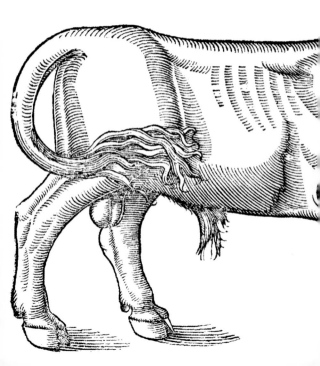

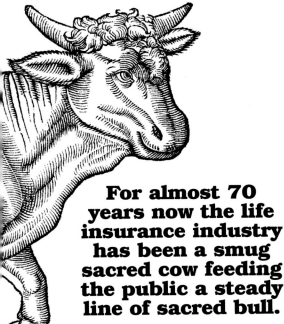

For almost 70 years now the life insurance industry has been a smug sacred cow feeding the public a steady line of sacred bull.

Ralph Nader (1934-), US
consumer-rights activist and
presidential candidate

123

FACTORY MEAT

**Most of the rich world's meat – and an
increasing amount of the world's fish – is
now produced in factory farms.**

**Here are just a few of the most common
methods used to bring your pork, fish
or fowl to the supermarket shelves and
butchers' hooks.**

SOW STALLS
**Having been 'served' on a 'rape
rack', the female pig is tethered
in a metal-barred stall where she
is unable to take more than one
step backward or one step forward
during her entire pregnancy. She is
denied not only exercise but light,
fresh air and companionship. By nature scrupulously
clean, she is forced to lie in her own excreta. She
gives birth on a perforated metal floor. Her piglets
are ripped away from her at two weeks – naturally
they would have been weaned at two months. Five
days later she is taken out and put on the rape rack
where the cycle begins again.**

POULTRY BATTERIES
Kept in a dismal shed consisting of row upon row of wire cages, the battery chicken may never see daylight until it is taken for slaughter. Egg-laying hens are crammed into a tiny cage measuring only 45 by 50 centimetres. Their feet are deformed by the sloping wire mesh floor. Even eating causes pain as feathers are rubbed away in attempts to reach the automatic feeder. Overcrowding and intense boredom and disease lead to aggression, cannibalism and neurotic disorders including self-mutilation. Farmers guillotine the tops of their beaks to stop hens pecking each other to death.

FISH FARMS
Fish are kept in cramped underwater cages and fed fish pellets containing antibiotics. Before they are bled to death they are starved for several weeks, because it is less messy to gut a starved fish. About 20 per cent die from afflictions such as skin ulcerations, bacterial kidney infections and cancerous tumours.

It has been said that humans are rational animals. All my life I have been searching for evidence which could support this.

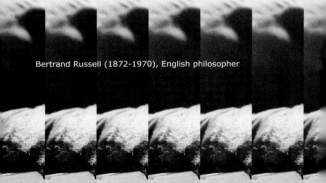

Bertrand Russell (1872-1970), English philosopher

126

In social matters,

pointless
conventions
are not

merely the **bee sting** of etiquette, but the **snake bite** of moral order.

Florence King (1936-), US novelist

129

DEMOCRACY MEANS GOVERNMENT BY DISCUSSION, BUT IT IS ONLY EFFECTIVE IF YOU CAN STOP PEOPLE TALKING.

Clement Attlee (1883-1967), British prime minister

Nearly all men can stand adversity, but if you want to test a man's character, give him power.

I am in favour of animal rights as well as human rights. That is the way of a whole human being.

Both quotations by Abraham Lincoln (1809-1865), US president

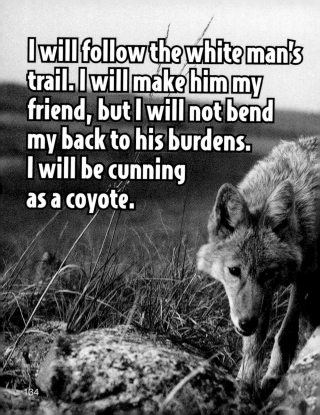

I will follow the white man's trail. I will make him my friend, but I will not bend my back to his burdens. I will be cunning as a coyote.

I will ask him to help me understand his ways, then I will prepare the way for my children, and their children. The Great Spirit has shown me – a day will come when they will outrun the white man in his own shoes.

Many Horses (late 19th century), Teton Lakota chief

You have all the characteristics of a popular politician: a horrible voice, bad breeding, and a vulgar manner.

Aristophanes (450-388 BCE), Greek dramatist

Nail polish or false eyelashes isn't politics. If you have good politics, what you wear is irrelevant. I don't take dictation from the pig-o-cratic style-setters who say I should dress like a middle-aged colored lady. My politics don't depend on whether my tits are in or out of a bra.

Florynce R Kennedy (1916-2001), African-American lawyer and civil-rights activist

Democracy is the recurrent suspicion that more than half of the people are right more than half the time.

EB White (1899-1985), US novelist

Politicians are like monkeys. The higher they climb the tree, the more revolting are the parts they expose.

Gwilym Lloyd George (1894-1967), son of Britain's World War One Prime Minister. He said this while he was an undergraduate but later climbed the tree himself, becoming an MP and government minister.

THE ZOO IS JUST NOT ENOUGH FOR ANIMALS OR PEOPLE. IN DEMEANING ANIMALS, WE DEMEAN OURSELVES. HOW MUCH LONGER IS THE TIGER GOING TO HAVE TO LIE ON ITS SLAB OF CONCRETE? HOW MUCH LONGER ARE WE GOING TO DRAG CHILDREN PAST THIS 3-D VERSION OF THEIR STORYBOOK CHARACTER AND URGE THEM TO WAVE AT ITS TAIL?

Tess Lemmon (1948-1992), English primate expert

Poverty is like a lion. If you do not fight, you get eaten.

Haya (Tanzanian) proverb

145

A whitewashed crow won't stay white for long.

Chinese proverb

The crow does not hide its prey,
but calls for others to share it;
So wealth will be with those of a
like disposition.

Tiruvalluvar (c.5th century),
Tamil sage poet

I FEEL VERY DEEPLY ABOUT VEGETARIANISM AND THE ANIMAL KINGDOM. IT WAS MY DOG BOYCOTT WHO LED ME TO QUESTION THE RIGHT OF HUMANS TO EAT OTHER SENTIENT BEINGS.

Cesar Chavez (1927-1993),
Mexican-American labour organizer

149

It always seems to me when the anti-suffrage members of the Government criticize militancy in women that it is very like BEASTS OF PREY reproaching gentler animals who turn in desperate resistance when at the point of death.

Emmeline Pankhurst
(1858-1928), English suffragist leader

EVERY **COUNTRY**

HAS THE

GOVERNMENT

IT **DESERVES**.

Joseph de Maistre (1753-1821), French writer

154

If you are neutral in situations of injustice, you have chosen the side of the oppressor. If an elephant has its foot on the tail of a mouse and you say that you are neutral, the mouse will not appreciate your neutrality.

Desmond Tutu (1931-), South African Archbishop

THE EXTINCTION FILES

One of the better-known species we have driven to the edge of oblivion.

Chinese Alligator
(Alligator sinensis)

HABITAT: This small alligator lives in the wetlands of Anhui (lower Yangtze valley), Zhejiang and Jiangsu provinces of China. A semi-aquatic reptile, it eats mainly snails, freshwater mussels, fish, insects and small mammals. It hibernates in the winter in burrows in the damp earth.

NUMBERS: Estimated at 500 in the wild. But there are many more in captive populations.

THREAT: Habitat destruction and intentional extermination by expanding human populations. During the flood season many alligators drown while hibernating. Severe drought destroys their wetland homes.

CONSERVATION: Protected by the Chinese Government. There are alligator-rearing centres in Anhui and outside China.

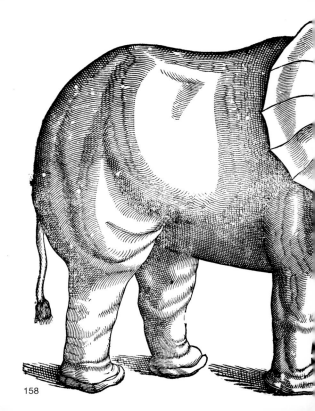

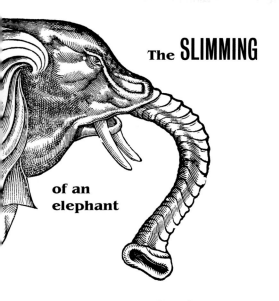

The **SLIMMING**

of an
elephant

and the losses of a rich man are
not noticeable.

Amharic (Ethiopian) proverb

There is nothing in which the birds differ more from humans than the way in which they can build and yet leave a landscape as it was before.

Robert Lynd
(1892-1970), US
sociologist

You always strain tuh be de bell cow, never be de tail uh nothin'.

Zora Neale Hurston
(1891-1960),
African-American
novelist

Take hope from the
heart of a man,

and you make him a beast of prey.

Louise de la Ramée, aka 'Ouida'
(1839-1908), English novelist

163

When the character
of a person is not
clear to you,

LOOK

at their friends.

Japanese Proverb

166

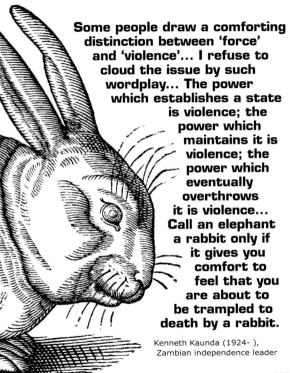

Some people draw a comforting distinction between 'force' and 'violence'... I refuse to cloud the issue by such wordplay... The power which establishes a state is violence; the power which maintains it is violence; the power which eventually overthrows it is violence... Call an elephant a rabbit only if it gives you comfort to feel that you are about to be trampled to death by a rabbit.

Kenneth Kaunda (1924-),
Zambian independence leader

167

Be mild with the mild, shrewd with the crafty, confiding to the honest, rough to the ruffian, and a thunderbolt to the liar. But in all this, never be unmindful of your own dignity.

John Brown (1800-1859), US antislavery activist

WHEN THE POLITICAL columnists say 'Every thinking man' they mean themselves,

and when candidates appeal to 'Every intelligent voter' they mean everybody who is going to vote for them.

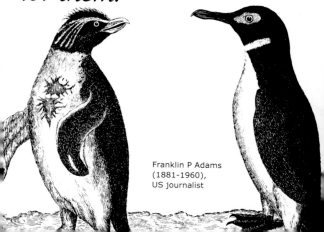

Franklin P Adams
(1881-1960),
US journalist

The animals of the planet are in desperate peril... Without free animal life I believe we will lose the spiritual equivalent of oxygen.

Alice Walker (1944-), African-American writer

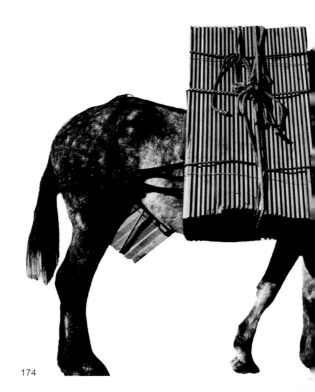

The marvel of
all history is
the patience
with which
men and
women
submit to
burdens
unnecessarily laid upon
them by their governments.

William H Borah

I AM NOT
BUSH, LION,
SAVAGERY
MINE ARE THE
SINEWS WHICH
BUILT YOUR CITIES
MY SONS FIGHTING
YOUR WARS
GAVE YOU VICTORY,
PRESTIGE

Grace
Akello
(1950-),
Ugandan poet
and politician

The trouble with the rat race is that even if you win, you're still a RAT.

Lily Tomlin (1939-),
US actor

179

The cocks may crow, but it's the hen that lays the egg.

Margaret Thatcher (1925-), British prime minister

In politics you must always keep running with the pack. The moment that you falter and they sense that you are injured, the rest will turn on you like wolves.

RA Butler (1902-1982),
British politician

183

A man is the only creature that consumes without producing. He does not give milk, he does not lay eggs, he is too weak to pull the plough, he cannot run fast enough to catch rabbits. Yet he is lord of all the animals. He sets them to work, he gives back to them the bare minimum that will prevent them from starving, and the rest he keeps for himself.

George Orwell (1903-1950),
English novelist and essayist

185

JUST SOME OF THE MANY ANIMAL-RELATED CAMPAIGNING ORGANIZATIONS...

INTERNATIONAL
Eurogroup for Animal Welfare
www.eurogroupanimalwelfare.org
International Fund for Animal Welfare 411 Main Street, PO Box 193, Yarmouth Port, MA 02675, US. tel: +1 508 744 2000. fax: +1 508 744 2009. email: info@ifaw.org web: www.ifaw.org
International Vegetarian Union www.ivu.org
World Conservation Union (IUCN) Rue Mauverney 28, Gland 1196, Switzerland. tel: +41 22 999 0000 email: mail@iucn.org web: www.iucn.org
World Society for the Protection of Animals [campaigns for a Universal Declaration for the Welfare of Animals], 89 Albert Embankment, London SE1 7TP, England. tel: +44 20 7793 5000. fax: +44 20 7793 02 08. email: declaration@wspa.org.uk web: www.wspa-international.org
WWF International [national organizations in all the countries below], Avenue du Mont Blanc, Gland 1196, Switzerland. tel: +41 22 364 9111 web: www.panda.org

AUSTRALIA
Animals Australia 37 O'Connell Street, North Melbourne, Vic 3051. tel: 1800 888 584 / 03 9329 6333
email: enquiries@animalsaustralia.org
Australian Animal Protection Society 10 Homeleigh Road, Keysborough, Vic 3173. tel: 03 9798 8415 web: www.aaps.org.au
Australian Vegetarian Society PO Box 56, Surry Hills NSW 2010.

tel: 02 9698 4339 email: avs@veg-soc.org web: www.veg-soc.org
Australian Wildlife Protection Council, 247 Flinders Lane, Melbourne, Vic 3000. tel: 03 9650 8326 web: www.awpc.org.au
RSPCA Australia PO Box 265, Deakin West, ACT 2600. tel: 02 6282 8300 web: www.rspca.org.au
Vegan Society of Australia email: info@veganaustralia.org web: www.veganaustralia.org
World League for the Protection of Animals PO Box 211, Gladesville, NSW 2111. tel: 02 9817 4892 email: info@wlpa.org

BRITAIN
Animal Aid The Old Chapel, Bradford Street, Tonbridge, Kent, TN9 1AW. Tel: 01732 364546 email: info@animalaid.org.uk web:www.animalaid.org.uk
British Union for the Abolition of Vivisection 16a Crane Grove, Islington, London N7 8NN. tel: 020 7700 4888. email: info@buav.org web: www.buav.org
Compassion in World Farming Charles House, 5a Charles Street, Petersfield, Hants, GU32 3EH. tel: 01730 264208 web: www.ciwf.org.uk
International Fund for Animal Welfare 87-90 Albert Embankment, London SE1 9UD. tel: 020 7587 6700 email: info-uk@ifaw.org
Royal Society for the Prevention of Cruelty to Animals Wilberforce Way, Southwater, West Sussex RH13 9RS. tel: 01403 821 000 email: international@rspca.org.uk web: www.rspca.org.uk
Vegan Society Donald Watson House, 7 Battle Rd, St Leonards-on-Sea, East Sussex TN37 7AA. tel: 0845 4588244 web: www.vegansociety.com

Vegetarian Society Parkdale, Dunham Road, Altrincham, Cheshire, England WA14 4QG. tel: 0161 925 2000
web: www.vegsoc.org

CANADA
Animal Rights Canada www.animalrightscanada.com
Calgary Vegetarian Society Suite 505, 918 16 Ave NW, Calgary AB, T2M 0K3. tel: 403 261 9628
email: info@calgaryveg.com web: calgaryveg.com
Global Action Network 372 St Catherine's St W, Suite 308, Montreal QC, H3B 1A2. tel: 514 939 5525
web: www.gan.ca/en/
Toronto Vegetarian Association 17 Baldwin St, 2nd floor, Toronto, ON M5T 1L1. tel: 416 544 9800 email: tva@veg.ca
web: www.veg.ca
International Fund for Animal Welfare Suite 612, 1 Nicholas St, Ottawa, ON K1N 7B7. tel: 613 241 8996 email: info-ca@ifaw.org

IRELAND
Compassion in World Farming Salmon Weir, Hanover St, Cork.
tel: 021 4272441 web: www.ciwf.ie
Irish Society for the Prevention of Cruelty to Animals
National Animal Centre, Derryglogher Lodge, Keenagh, Co Longford. tel: 043 25035 email: info@ispca.ie web: www.ispca.ie
Vegetarian Society of Ireland PO Box 3010, Dublin 4. email: vegsoc@ireland.com web: www.vegetarian.ie

NEW ZEALAND/ AOTEAROA
Green Party Animal Welfare Campaign
www.greens.org.nz/ campaigns/ animalwelfare

Royal NZ Society for the Prevention of Cruelty to Animals
PO Box 15349, New Lynn, Auckland 7. tel: 09 827 6094
email: info@rnzspca.org.nz web: www.rspcanz.org.nz
SAFE Level 1, 196 Hereford St, PO Box 13 366, Christchurch.
tel: 03 379 9711 email: safe@safe.org.nz web: www.safe.org.nz
Vegan Society of New Zealand www.veganz.pl.net
Vegetarian Society of New Zealand PO Box 26664, Epsom,
Auckland. Tel: 09 523 4686 email: nzvs@ivu.org
web: www.ivu.org/nzvs/

UNITED STATES
American Society for the Prevention of Cruelty to Animals
424 E 92nd St, New York, NY 10128-6804. tel: 212 876 7700
web: www.aspca.org
American Vegan Society 56 Dinshah Lane, PO Box 369,
Malaga NJ 08328. tel: 856 694 2887
web: www.americanvegan.org
Animal Protection Institute of America PO Box 22505,
Sacramento, CA 95822. tel: 916 447 3085
email: info@api4animals.org web: www.api4animals.org
Animal Rights International PO Box 532, Woodbury, CT
06798. tel: 203 263 8532 email: info@ari-online.org
web: www.ari-online.org
Animal Welfare Institute PO Box 3650, Washington, DC
20027. tel: 703 836 4300 web: www.animalwelfare.com
Vegetarian Union of North America PO Box 9710,
Washington, DC 20016. email: vuna@ivu.org
web: www.ivu.org/vuna

More wit, wisdom and inspiration from the New Internationalist BOOKS TO GO...

'The highest expression of dignity can be summed up in the single word "No!" – being able to say "No!" when you disagree.'

Dai Qing (contemporary), Chinese journalist and campaigner against China's Three Gorges Dam project

'True peace is not merely the absence of tension: it is the presence of justice.'

Martin Luther King Jr (1929-1968), African-American leader.

ORDER ONLINE AT: www.newint.org/shop

New Internationalist Publications is a co-operative with offices in Oxford (England), Adelaide (Australia), Toronto (Canada) and Christchurch (New Zealand/Aotearoa). It exists to report on the issues of world poverty and inequality; to focus attention on the unjust relationship between the powerful and powerless in both rich and poor nations; to debate and campaign for the radical changes necessary within and between those nations if the basic material and spiritual needs of all are to be met; and to bring to life the people, the ideas, the action in the fight for global justice.

The monthly **New Internationalist** magazine now has more than 75,000 subscribers worldwide. In addition to the magazine, the co-operative publishes the One World Calendar and the One World Almanac, outstanding collections of full-colour photographs. It also publishes books, including: the successful series of No-Nonsense Guides to the key issues in the world today; cookbooks containing recipes and cultural information from around the world; and photographic books on topics such as Nomadic Peoples and Water. The **NI** is the English-language publisher of the biennial reference book *The World Guide*, written by the Instituto del Tercer Mundo in Uruguay.

The co-operative is financially independent but aims to break even; any surpluses are reinvested so as to bring New Internationalist publications to as many people as possible.

www.newint.org